CLIENT RECOVERY JOURNAL

THE NEW NORMAL

HOW LIFE HAS CHANGED

MATTHEW A. LATHROP

WORD ASSOCIATION PUBLISHERS
www.wordassociation.com
1.800.827.7903

Printed in the United States of America.

ISBN: 978-1-63385-365-2

Designed and published by
Word Association Publishers
205 Fifth Avenue
Tarentum, Pennsylvania 15084

www.wordassociation.com
1.800.827.7903

INTRODUCTION

Over the years of helping clients, like you, with injury claims, we have found it helpful to our clients to have a book where they can keep track of their symptoms, doctor visits, and recovery. The purpose of this document is to create a single place to track all this information, to pass on to this office when we meet or speak by phone to collect regular or unscheduled updates on your treatment, symptoms and recovery. We ask that you have this book handy at any time we meet or confer to discuss your case.

Believe it or not, many of them forget just what it was like during the process of getting better, after the passage of time. This book is designed with the goal of providing you with one place where you can track your symptoms, doctor visits and recovery in an orderly way. The purpose of the book is to create, for this office, your written communication about these elements of your claim.

You should treat this as written communication with your lawyer.

We will be using this information, just like we would a phone call to us to discuss these same topics. We will be using it to further your claim against the defendant and his or her or its insurance company.

Having this book at your nightstand, or by your telephone is the most common place to keep it, so you know where it is at all times.

Don't worry about what condition it is in, at the end: coffee stains, dirt, spills… we don't care. We just want to make sure that we understand everything about your injury, symptoms, doctor visits, and recovery, from beginning to end.

This book makes sure you are keeping track of what we need to know.

Many of our clients, when they reach the nine-month post-injury recovery point, begin to hear from their doctor that treatment is probably coming to an end. This does not mean that you are "back to normal." It simply means that your doctor is running out of options to help with your recovery. This is a general statement, and of course may occur sooner or later than the nine-month mark.

This is an important point in your recovery, however. When your doctor begins to discuss an end of active treatment, **it is critical that you let this office know.** At this stage, we need to review your treatment and progress, and discuss with you the next steps in your case against the insurance company.

If your doctor suggests that "you will probably be done/released/discharged after the next visit", please call our office immediately. This is helpful for moving your case along, as efficiently as possible.

PERSONAL INJURY JOURNAL

INSTRUCTIONS

Witnesses Table:

Please list below any people who know you well; who have known you since before your injury; who could tell us about the changes they have seen in your work, your home life, your social activities, or any time your injury affected day-to-day activities. If possible, tell us about a specific event that this person witnessed and could describe to us.

Think not just of family, but also people in the community with whom you regularly interact: your barber or stylist; your kid's teachers and/or coaches; members of teams or clubs to which you belong; co-workers; supervisors; customers whom you see at work regularly. Think creatively!

These witnesses are some of the most important people for proving how your injury affects you. We encourage you to include as many people as come to mind. When the time comes to interview them, we will discuss it with you first – no surprises! Then, we will interview them and determine if they can help or not. Let us worry about putting together the best evidence possible.

Name	Address	Phone No.	What do they know?

INSTRUCTIONS:

Periodically, we would like you to complete this pain questionnaire ***for our records***. Think of this as a written form for updating your lawyer. Please complete each two-page questionnaire at the time frame in your recovery indicated and fill in the date you completed the form. This will be a very important document to help tell the story of your journey to recovery.

Date:____________________

PAIN SCALE

Mark on the line the level of pain you are experiencing RIGHT now.

No pain 0 ____ **10 Worst pain Imaginable**

Mark on the line the average level of pain since your last report.

No pain 0 ____ **10 Worst pain imaginable**

Mark areas of *PAIN* that you have on the diagram using **SHADING**

Mark areas of *TINGLING or PINS AND NEEDLES* with **CROSSES**

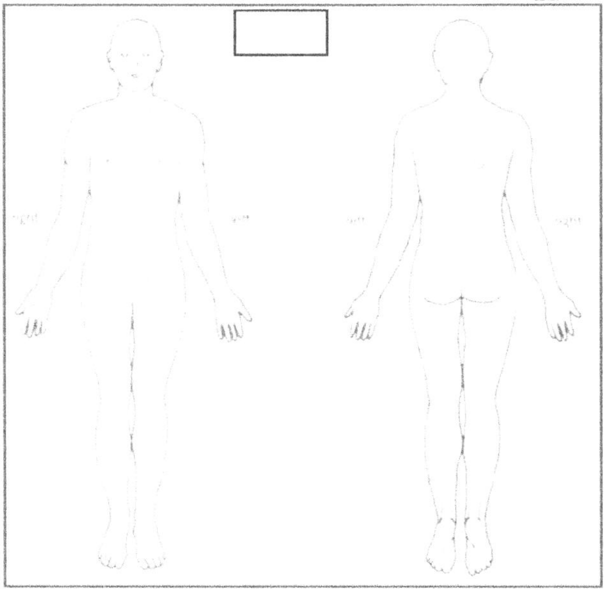

PLEASE ANSWER EACH OF THESE QUESTIONS AT THE SAME TIME AS YOU COMPLETE THE PAIN QUESTIONNAIRE ON THE PREVIOUS PAGE:

"Have you returned to work?" Yes No

On what date?______________________________

Full duty? Yes No

Has a doctor given you any restrictions? (list)

____

____

____

____

____

____

"What has helped with the pain?"

____

____

____

"What has made it worse?"

____

____

____

DOCTOR VISIT PREPARATION RECORD

(Before your next doctor visit, fill this out. Take it with you!)

Date______________________________

Doctor/facility: ____

____

Reason for visit: ____

____

How are you feeling today?

(LIST ALL AREAS OF PAIN; DESCRIBE PROBLEMS WITH SLEEP, HEADACHES, ANXIETY, STRESS, FEAR, FLASHBACKS, INTRUSIVE THOUGHTS)

____

____

____

How did your injuries affect your job, *since your last visit to this doctor*?

____

____

How did your injuries affect your household duties or family life *since your last visit to this doctor*?

____

____

Did you miss any events or social activities because of your injuries since your last visit?

____

____

Did you incur any costs as a result of the visit to this doctor, or his recommendations/ prescriptions?

____

____

Was any testing done or ordered on this visit? (X-rays, blood work, etc.?)

____

____

What treatments were given or prescribed on this visit?

____

____

Recommendations for more care and/or follow up? With whom?

____

____

Other notes:

____

____

Things to do:

ONE WEEK AFTER INJURY

Date:______________________

Mark on the line the level of pain you are experiencing RIGHT now.

No pain 0 ______________________ **10 Worst pain Imaginable**

Mark on the line the average level of pain since your last report.

No pain 0 ______________________ **10 Worst pain imaginable**

PAIN DIAGRAM

Mark areas of *PAIN* that you have on the diagram using **SHADING**

Mark areas of *TINGLING or PINS AND NEEDLES* with **CROSSES**

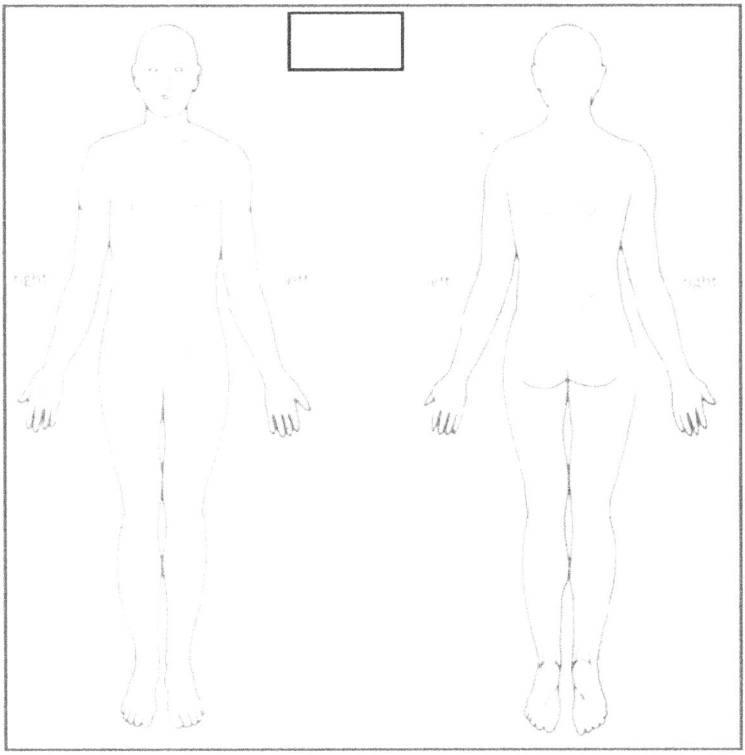

PLEASE ANSWER EACH OF THESE QUESTIONS AT THE SAME TIME AS YOU COMPLETE THE PAIN QUESTIONNAIRE ON THE PREVIOUS PAGE:

"Have you returned to work?" Yes No

On what date?______________________________

Full duty? Yes No

Has a doctor given you any restrictions? (list)

____

____

____

____

____

____

"What has helped with the pain?"

____

____

____

"What has made it worse?"

____

____

____

DOCTOR VISIT PREPARATION RECORD

(Before your next doctor visit, fill this out. Take it with you!)

Date____________________________

Doctor/facility: ____

____

Reason for visit: ____

____

How are you feeling today?

(LIST ALL AREAS OF PAIN; DESCRIBE PROBLEMS WITH SLEEP, HEADACHES, ANXIETY, STRESS, FEAR, FLASHBACKS, INTRUSIVE THOUGHTS)

____

____

____

How did your injuries affect your job, *since your last visit to this doctor*?

____

____

How did your injuries affect your household duties or family life *since your last visit to this doctor*?

____

____

Did you miss any events or social activities because of your injuries since your last visit?

____

____

Did you incur any costs as a result of the visit to this doctor, or his recommendations/ prescriptions?

____

____

Was any testing done or ordered on this visit? (X-rays, blood work, etc.?)

____

____

What treatments were given or prescribed on this visit?

____

____

Recommendations for more care and/or follow up? With whom?

____

____

Other notes:

____

____

Things to do:

TWO WEEKS AFTER INJURY

Date:_________________________

Mark on the line the level of pain you are experiencing RIGHT now.

No pain 0 ____ **10 Worst pain Imaginable**

Mark on the line the average level of pain since your last report.

No pain 0 ____ **10 Worst pain imaginable**

PAIN DIAGRAM

Mark areas of *PAIN* that you have on the diagram using **SHADING**

Mark areas of *TINGLING or PINS AND NEEDLES* with **CROSSES**

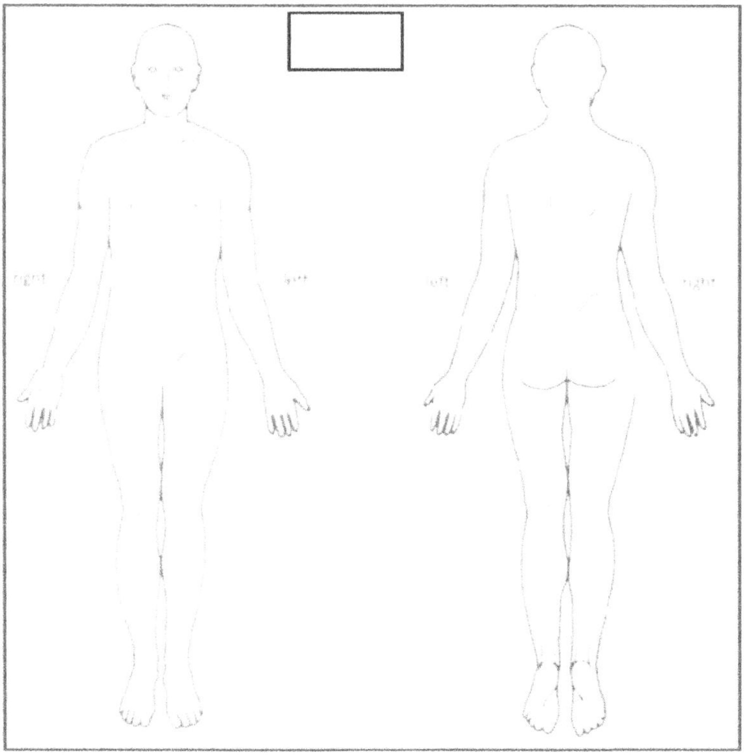

PLEASE ANSWER EACH OF THESE QUESTIONS AT THE SAME TIME AS YOU COMPLETE THE PAIN QUESTIONNAIRE ON THE PREVIOUS PAGE:

"Have you returned to work?" Yes No

On what date?____________________

Full duty? Yes No

Has a doctor given you any restrictions? (list)

____

____

____

____

____

____

"What has helped with the pain?"

____

____

____

"What has made it worse?"

____

____

____

DOCTOR VISIT PREPARATION RECORD

(Before your next doctor visit, fill this out. Take it with you!)

Date: ______________________

Doctor/facility: ______________________

____

Reason for visit: ______________________

____

How are you feeling today?

(LIST ALL AREAS OF PAIN; DESCRIBE PROBLEMS WITH SLEEP, HEADACHES, ANXIETY, STRESS, FEAR, FLASHBACKS, INTRUSIVE THOUGHTS)

____

____

____

How did your injuries affect your job, *since your last visit to this doctor*?

____

____

How did your injuries affect your household duties or family life *since your last visit to this doctor*?

____

____

Did you miss any events or social activities because of your injuries since your last visit?

Did you incur any costs as a result of the visit to this doctor, or his recommendations/prescriptions?

Was any testing done or ordered on this visit? (X-rays, blood work, etc.?)

What treatments were given or prescribed on this visit?

Recommendations for more care and/or follow up? With whom?

Other notes:

Things to do:

THREE WEEKS AFTER INJURY

Date:______________________

Mark on the line the level of pain you are experiencing RIGHT now.

No pain 0 ________________________________ **10 Worst pain Imaginable**

Mark on the line the average level of pain since your last report.

No pain 0 ________________________________ **10 Worst pain imaginable**

PAIN DIAGRAM

Mark areas of *PAIN* that you have on the diagram using **SHADING**

Mark areas of *TINGLING or PINS AND NEEDLES* with **CROSSES**

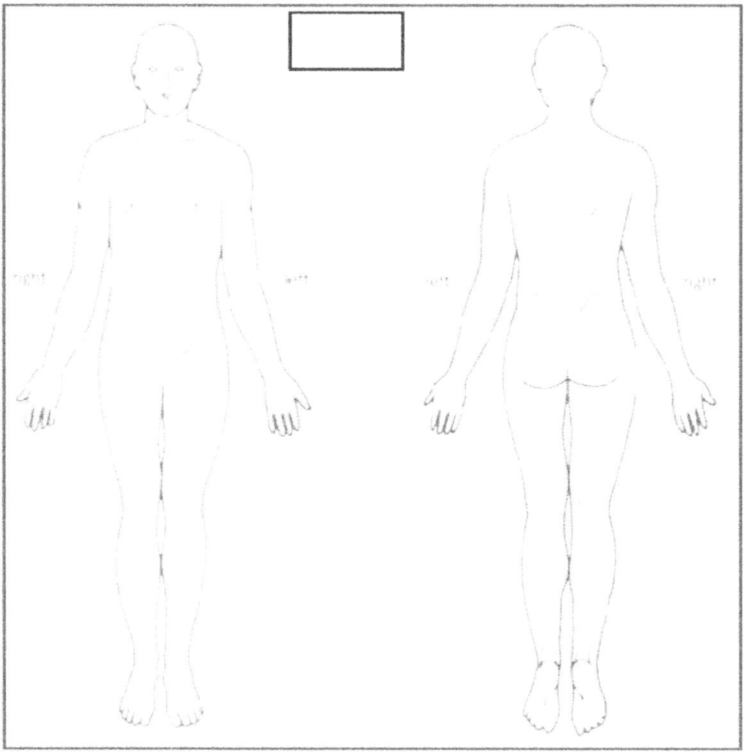

PLEASE ANSWER EACH OF THESE QUESTIONS AT THE SAME TIME AS YOU COMPLETE THE PAIN QUESTIONNAIRE ON THE PREVIOUS PAGE:

"Have you returned to work?" Yes No

On what date?______________________________

Full duty? Yes No

Has a doctor given you any restrictions? (list)

____

____

____

____

____

____

"What has helped with the pain?"

____

____

____

"What has made it worse?"

____

____

____

DOCTOR VISIT PREPARATION RECORD

(Before your next doctor visit, fill this out. Take it with you!)

Date:______________________________

Doctor/facility: ____

____

Reason for visit: ____

____

How are you feeling today?

(*LIST ALL AREAS OF PAIN; DESCRIBE PROBLEMS WITH SLEEP, HEADACHES, ANXIETY, STRESS, FEAR, FLASHBACKS, INTRUSIVE THOUGHTS)*

____

____

____

How did your injuries affect your job, *since your last visit to this doctor*?

____

____

How did your injuries affect your household duties or family life *since your last visit to this doctor*?

____

____

Did you miss any events or social activities because of your injuries since your last visit?

____

____

Did you incur any costs as a result of the visit to this doctor, or his recommendations/ prescriptions?

____

____

Was any testing done or ordered on this visit? (X-rays, blood work, etc.?)

____

____

What treatments were given or prescribed on this visit?

____

____

Recommendations for more care and/or follow up? With whom?

____

____

Other notes:

____

____

Things to do:

FOUR WEEKS AFTER INJURY

Date:______________________

Mark on the line the level of pain you are experiencing RIGHT now.

No pain 0 ______________________________ **10 Worst pain Imaginable**

Mark on the line the average level of pain since your last report.

No pain 0 ______________________________ **10 Worst pain imaginable**

PAIN DIAGRAM

Mark areas of *PAIN* that you have on the diagram using **SHADING**

Mark areas of *TINGLING or PINS AND NEEDLES* with **CROSSES**

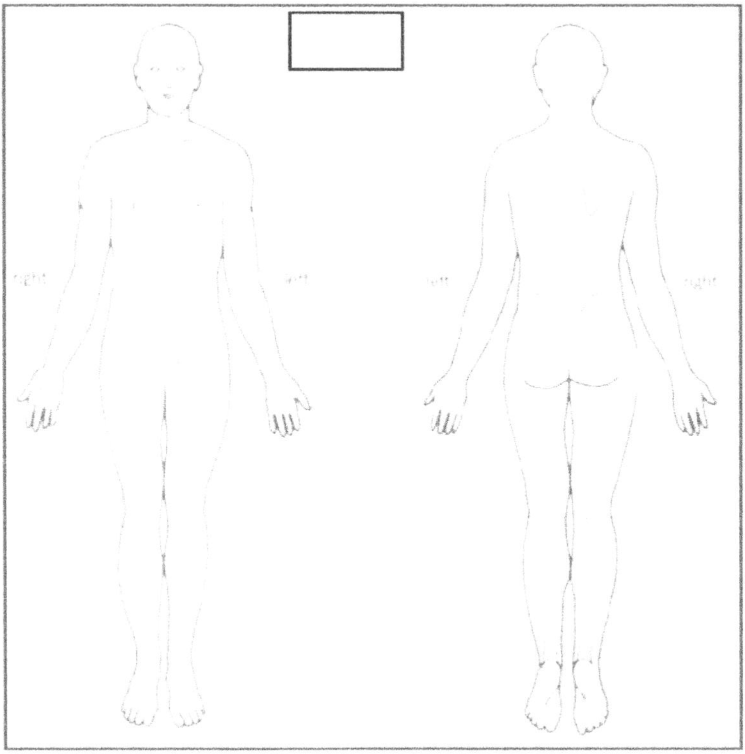

PLEASE ANSWER EACH OF THESE QUESTIONS AT THE SAME TIME AS YOU COMPLETE THE PAIN QUESTIONNAIRE ON THE PREVIOUS PAGE:

"Have you returned to work?" Yes No

On what date?________________________

Full duty? Yes No

Has a doctor given you any restrictions? (list)

____

____

____

____

____

____

"What has helped with the pain?"

____

____

____

"What has made it worse?"

____

____

____

DOCTOR VISIT PREPARATION RECORD

(Before your next doctor visit, fill this out. Take it with you!)

Date:______________________________

Doctor/facility: ____

____

Reason for visit: ____

____

How are you feeling today?

(LIST ALL AREAS OF PAIN; DESCRIBE PROBLEMS WITH SLEEP, HEADACHES, ANXIETY, STRESS, FEAR, FLASHBACKS, INTRUSIVE THOUGHTS)

____

____

____

How did your injuries affect your job, *since your last visit to this doctor*?

____

____

How did your injuries affect your household duties or family life *since your last visit to this doctor*?

____

____

Did you miss any events or social activities because of your injuries since your last visit?

____

____

Did you incur any costs as a result of the visit to this doctor, or his recommendations/ prescriptions?

____

____

Was any testing done or ordered on this visit? (X-rays, blood work, etc.?)

____

____

What treatments were given or prescribed on this visit?

____

____

Recommendations for more care and/or follow up? With whom?

____

____

Other notes:

____

____

Things to do:

TWO MONTHS AFTER INJURY

Date:________________________

Mark on the line the level of pain you are experiencing RIGHT now.

No pain 0 ______________________________ **10 Worst pain Imaginable**

Mark on the line the average level of pain since your last report.

No pain 0 ______________________________ **10 Worst pain imaginable**

PAIN DIAGRAM

Mark areas of *PAIN* that you have on the diagram using **SHADING**

Mark areas of *TINGLING or PINS AND NEEDLES* with **CROSSES**

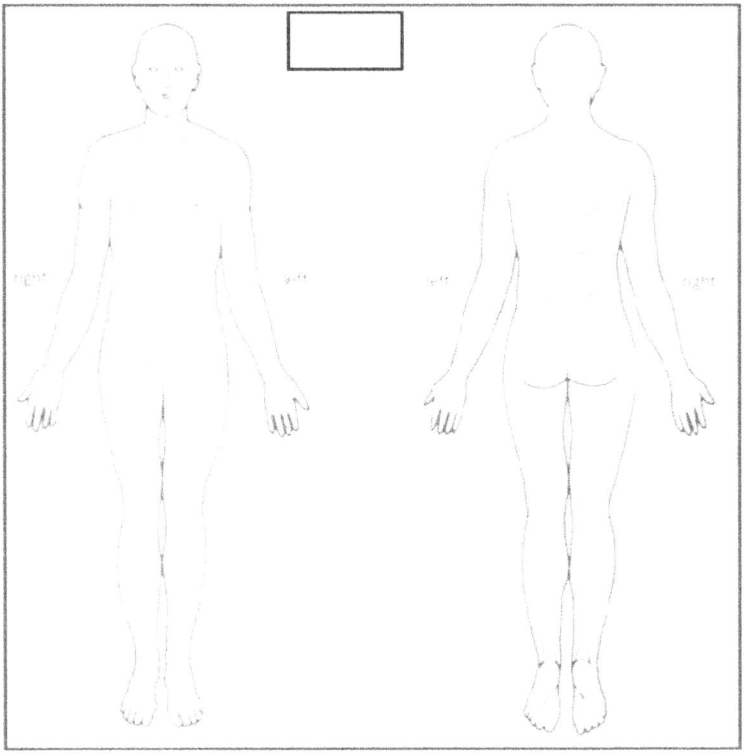

PLEASE ANSWER EACH OF THESE QUESTIONS AT THE SAME TIME AS YOU COMPLETE THE PAIN QUESTIONNAIRE ON THE PREVIOUS PAGE:

"Have you returned to work?" Yes No

On what date?______________________________

Full duty? Yes No

Has a doctor given you any restrictions? (list)

____

____

____

____

____

____

"What has helped with the pain?"

____

____

____

"What has made it worse?"

____

____

____

DOCTOR VISIT PREPARATION RECORD

(Before your next doctor visit, fill this out. Take it with you!)

Date:____________________________

Doctor/facility: ____

____

Reason for visit: ____

____

How are you feeling today?

(LIST ALL AREAS OF PAIN; DESCRIBE PROBLEMS WITH SLEEP, HEADACHES, ANXIETY, STRESS, FEAR, FLASHBACKS, INTRUSIVE THOUGHTS)

____

____

____

How did your injuries affect your job, *since your last visit to this doctor*?

____

____

How did your injuries affect your household duties or family life *since your last visit to this doctor*?

____

____

Did you miss any events or social activities because of your injuries since your last visit?

____

____

Did you incur any costs as a result of the visit to this doctor, or his recommendations/ prescriptions?

____

____

Was any testing done or ordered on this visit? (X-rays, blood work, etc.?)

____

____

What treatments were given or prescribed on this visit?

____

____

Recommendations for more care and/or follow up? With whom?

____

____

Other notes:

____

____

Things to do:

THREE MONTHS AFTER INJURY

Date:________________________

Mark on the line the level of pain you are experiencing RIGHT now.

No pain 0 ____ **10 Worst pain Imaginable**

Mark on the line the average level of pain since your last report.

No pain 0 ____ **10 Worst pain imaginable**

PAIN DIAGRAM

Mark areas of *PAIN* that you have on the diagram using **SHADING**

Mark areas of *TINGLING or PINS AND NEEDLES* with **CROSSES**

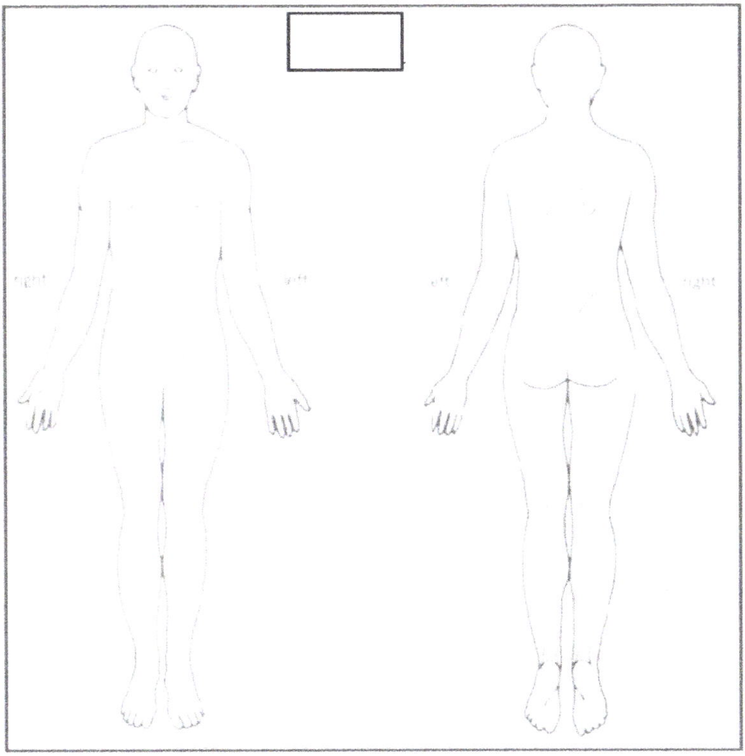

PLEASE ANSWER EACH OF THESE QUESTIONS AT THE SAME TIME AS YOU COMPLETE THE PAIN QUESTIONNAIRE ON THE PREVIOUS PAGE:

"Have you returned to work?" Yes No

On what date?______________________________

Full duty? Yes No

Has a doctor given you any restrictions? (list)

____

____

____

____

____

____

"What has helped with the pain?"

____

____

____

"What has made it worse?"

____

____

____

DOCTOR VISIT PREPARATION RECORD

(Before your next doctor visit, fill this out. Take it with you!)

Date:______________________________

Doctor/facility: ____

____

Reason for visit: ____

____

How are you feeling today?

(LIST ALL AREAS OF PAIN; DESCRIBE PROBLEMS WITH SLEEP, HEADACHES, ANXIETY, STRESS, FEAR, FLASHBACKS, INTRUSIVE THOUGHTS)

____

____

____

How did your injuries affect your job, *since your last visit to this doctor*?

____

____

How did your injuries affect your household duties or family life *since your last visit to this doctor*?

____

____

Did you miss any events or social activities because of your injuries since your last visit?

Did you incur any costs as a result of the visit to this doctor, or his recommendations/ prescriptions?

Was any testing done or ordered on this visit? (X-rays, blood work, etc.?)

What treatments were given or prescribed on this visit?

Recommendations for more care and/or follow up? With whom?

Other notes:

Things to do:

FOUR MONTHS AFTER INJURY

Date:____________________

Mark on the line the level of pain you are experiencing RIGHT now.

No pain 0 ________________________________ **10** **Worst pain Imaginable**

Mark on the line the average level of pain since your last report.

No pain 0 ________________________________ **10** **Worst pain imaginable**

PAIN DIAGRAM

Mark areas of *PAIN* that you have on the diagram using **SHADING**

Mark areas of *TINGLING or PINS AND NEEDLES* with **CROSSES**

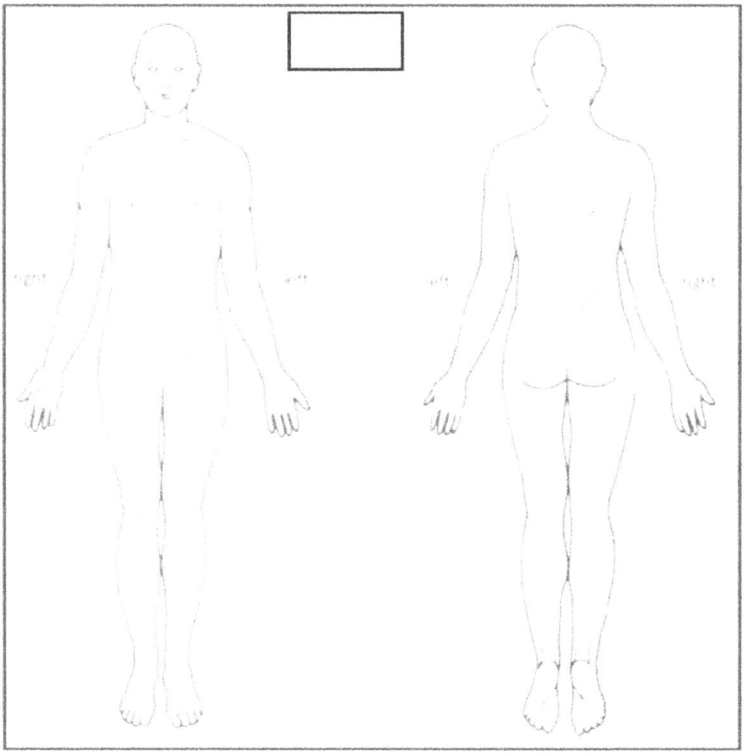

PLEASE ANSWER EACH OF THESE QUESTIONS AT THE SAME TIME AS YOU COMPLETE THE PAIN QUESTIONNAIRE ON THE PREVIOUS PAGE:

"Have you returned to work?" Yes No

On what date?______________________________

Full duty? Yes No

Has a doctor given you any restrictions? (list)

____

____

____

____

____

____

"What has helped with the pain?"

____

____

____

"What has made it worse?"

____

____

____

DOCTOR VISIT PREPARATION RECORD

(Before your next doctor visit, fill this out. Take it with you!)

Date: ______________________________

Doctor/facility: ____

____

Reason for visit: ____

____

How are you feeling today?

(LIST ALL AREAS OF PAIN; DESCRIBE PROBLEMS WITH SLEEP, HEADACHES, ANXIETY, STRESS, FEAR, FLASHBACKS, INTRUSIVE THOUGHTS)

____

____

____

How did your injuries affect your job, *since your last visit to this doctor*?

____

____

How did your injuries affect your household duties or family life *since your last visit to this doctor*?

____

____

Did you miss any events or social activities because of your injuries since your last visit?

____

____

Did you incur any costs as a result of the visit to this doctor, or his recommendations/ prescriptions?

____

____

Was any testing done or ordered on this visit? (X-rays, blood work, etc.?)

____

____

What treatments were given or prescribed on this visit?

____

____

Recommendations for more care and/or follow up? With whom?

____

____

Other notes:

____

____

Things to do:

FIVE MONTHS AFTER INJURY

Date:________________________

Mark on the line the level of pain you are experiencing RIGHT now.

No pain 0 .... **10 Worst pain Imaginable**

Mark on the line the average level of pain since your last report.

No pain 0 .... **10 Worst pain imaginable**

PAIN DIAGRAM

Mark areas of *PAIN* that you have on the diagram using **SHADING**

Mark areas of *TINGLING or PINS AND NEEDLES* with **CROSSES**

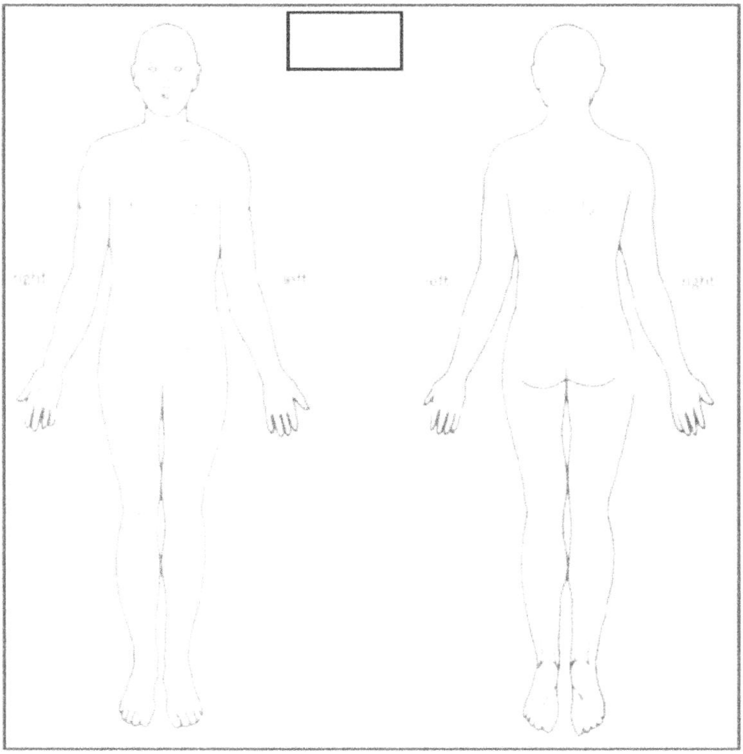

PLEASE ANSWER EACH OF THESE QUESTIONS AT THE SAME TIME AS YOU COMPLETE THE PAIN QUESTIONNAIRE ON THE PREVIOUS PAGE:

"Have you returned to work?" Yes No

On what date?______________________________

Full duty? Yes No

Has a doctor given you any restrictions? (list)

____

____

____

____

____

____

"What has helped with the pain?"

____

____

____

"What has made it worse?"

____

____

____

DOCTOR VISIT PREPARATION RECORD

(Before your next doctor visit, fill this out. Take it with you!)

Date: ______________________________

Doctor/facility: ____

____

Reason for visit: ____

____

How are you feeling today?

(*LIST ALL AREAS OF PAIN; DESCRIBE PROBLEMS WITH SLEEP, HEADACHES, ANXIETY, STRESS, FEAR, FLASHBACKS, INTRUSIVE THOUGHTS)*

____

____

____

How did your injuries affect your job, *since your last visit to this doctor*?

____

____

How did your injuries affect your household duties or family life *since your last visit to this doctor*?

____

____

Did you miss any events or social activities because of your injuries since your last visit?

____

____

Did you incur any costs as a result of the visit to this doctor, or his recommendations/ prescriptions?

____

____

Was any testing done or ordered on this visit? (X-rays, blood work, etc.?)

____

____

What treatments were given or prescribed on this visit?

____

____

Recommendations for more care and/or follow up? With whom?

____

____

Other notes:

____

____

Things to do:

SIX MONTHS AFER INJURY

Date:________________________

Mark on the line the level of pain you are experiencing RIGHT now.

No pain 0 ______________________________ **10 Worst pain Imaginable**

Mark on the line the average level of pain since your last report.

No pain 0 ______________________________ **10 Worst pain imaginable**

PAIN DIAGRAM

Mark areas of *PAIN* that you have on the diagram using **SHADING**

Mark areas of *TINGLING or PINS AND NEEDLES* with **CROSSES**

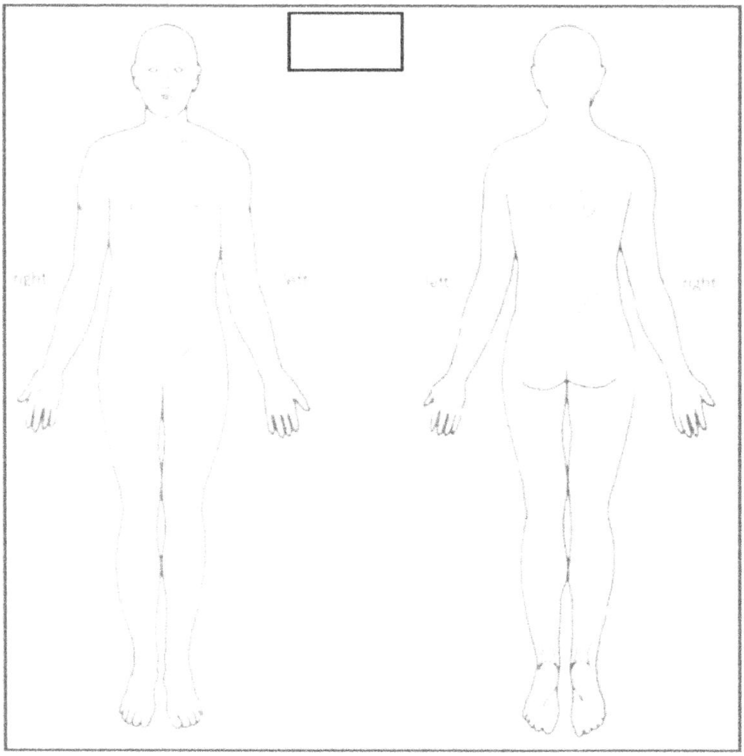

PLEASE ANSWER EACH OF THESE QUESTIONS AT THE SAME TIME AS YOU COMPLETE THE PAIN QUESTIONNAIRE ON THE PREVIOUS PAGE:

"Have you returned to work?" Yes No

On what date?____________________________

Full duty? Yes No

Has a doctor given you any restrictions? (list)

____

____

____

____

____

____

"What has helped with the pain?"

____

____

____

"What has made it worse?"

____

____

____

DOCTOR VISIT PREPARATION RECORD

(Before your next doctor visit, fill this out. Take it with you!)

Date: ______________________

Doctor/facility: ________________________________

____

Reason for visit: ______________________________

____

How are you feeling today?

(LIST ALL AREAS OF PAIN; DESCRIBE PROBLEMS WITH SLEEP, HEADACHES, ANXIETY, STRESS, FEAR, FLASHBACKS, INTRUSIVE THOUGHTS)

____

____

____

How did your injuries affect your job, *since your last visit to this doctor*?

____

____

How did your injuries affect your household duties or family life *since your last visit to this doctor*?

____

____

Did you miss any events or social activities because of your injuries since your last visit?

Did you incur any costs as a result of the visit to this doctor, or his recommendations/ prescriptions?

Was any testing done or ordered on this visit? (X-rays, blood work, etc.?)

What treatments were given or prescribed on this visit?

Recommendations for more care and/or follow up? With whom?

Other notes:

Things to do:

NINE MONTHS AFTER INJURY

Date:______________________

Mark on the line the level of pain you are experiencing RIGHT now.

No pain 0 ______________________________ **10 Worst pain Imaginable**

Mark on the line the average level of pain since your last report.

No pain 0 ______________________________ **10 Worst pain imaginable**

PAIN DIAGRAM

Mark areas of *PAIN* that you have on the diagram using **SHADING**

Mark areas of *TINGLING or PINS AND NEEDLES* with **CROSSES**

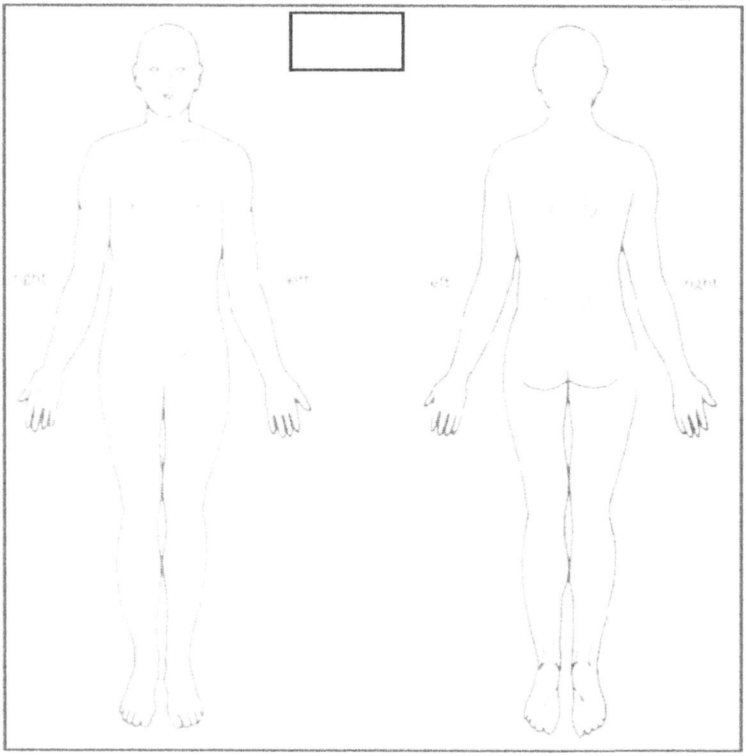

PLEASE ANSWER EACH OF THESE QUESTIONS AT THE SAME TIME AS YOU COMPLETE THE PAIN QUESTIONNAIRE ON THE PREVIOUS PAGE:

"Have you returned to work?" Yes No

On what date?______________________________

Full duty? Yes No

Has a doctor given you any restrictions? (list)

____

____

____

____

____

____

"What has helped with the pain?"

____

____

____

"What has made it worse?"

____

____

____

Many of our clients, when they reach the 9-month recovery point, begin to hear from their doctor that their treatment is probably coming to an end. This does not mean that you are "back to normal." It simply means that your doctors are running out of options to help with your recovery. This is a general statement, and of course may occur sooner or later than the 9-month mark.

This is an important point in your recovery, however. When your doctor begins to discuss an end of active treatment, **it is critical that you let this office know.** At this stage, we need to review your treatment and progress, and discuss with you the next steps in your case against the insurance company.

If your doctor suggests that "you will probably be done/ released/discharged after the next visit", please call our office immediately. This is helpful for moving your case along, as efficiently as possible.

DOCTOR VISIT PREPARATION RECORD

(Before your next doctor visit, fill this out. Take it with you!)

Date: ______________________________

Doctor/facility: ____

____

Reason for visit: ____

____

How are you feeling today?

(LIST ALL AREAS OF PAIN; DESCRIBE PROBLEMS WITH SLEEP, HEADACHES, ANXIETY, STRESS, FEAR, FLASHBACKS, INTRUSIVE THOUGHTS)

____

____

____

How did your injuries affect your job, *since your last visit to this doctor*?

____

____

How did your injuries affect your household duties or family life *since your last visit to this doctor*?

____

____

Did you miss any events or social activities because of your injuries since your last visit?

____

____

Did you incur any costs as a result of the visit to this doctor, or his recommendations/ prescriptions?

____

____

Was any testing done or ordered on this visit? (X-rays, blood work, etc.?)

____

____

What treatments were given or prescribed on this visit?

____

____

Recommendations for more care and/or follow up? With whom?

____

____

Other notes:

____

____

Things to do:

Notes: (Use this page for any other important notes you would like to discuss, with your lawyer):

WA

Made in the USA
Monee, IL
04 November 2026

67381844R10046